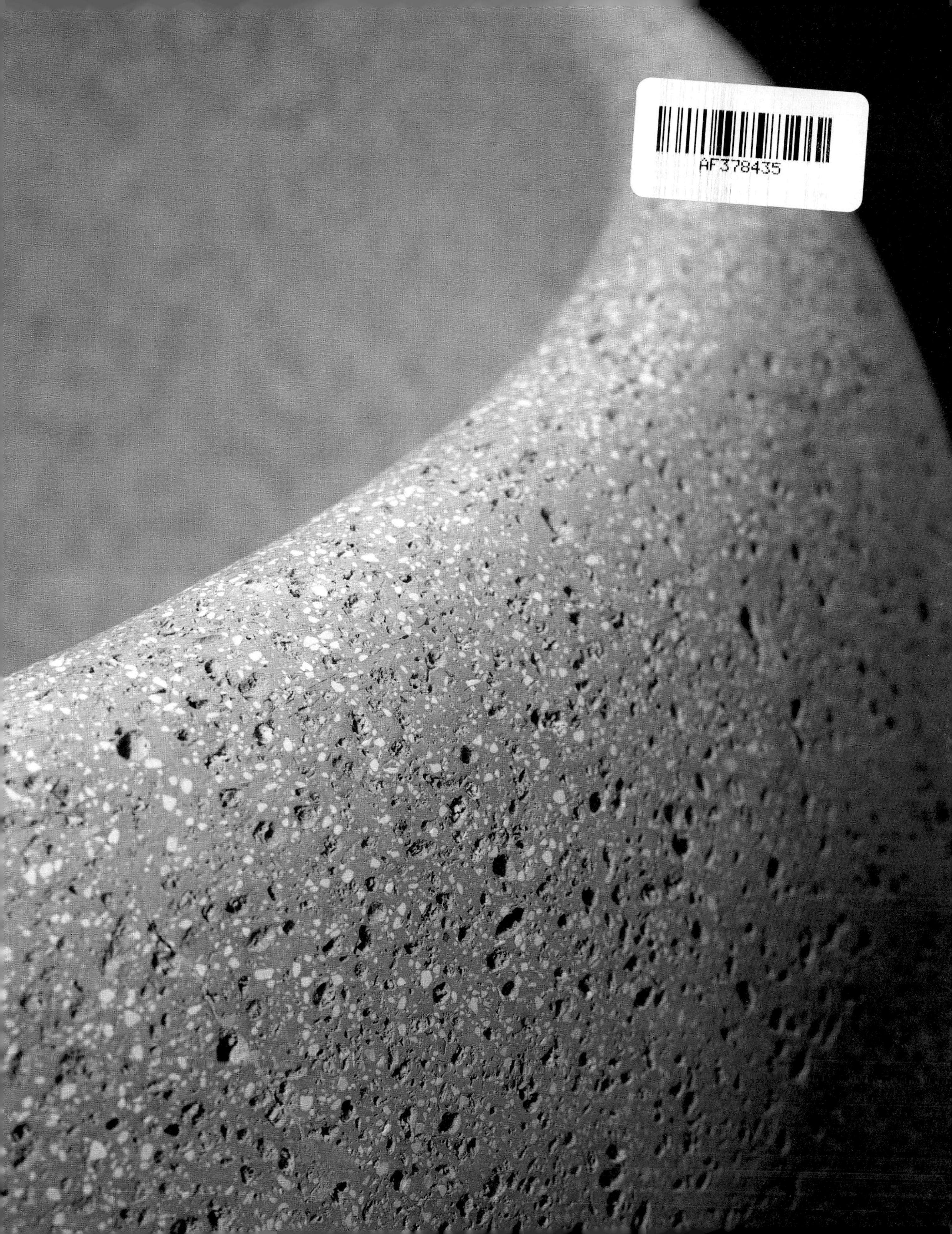
AF378435

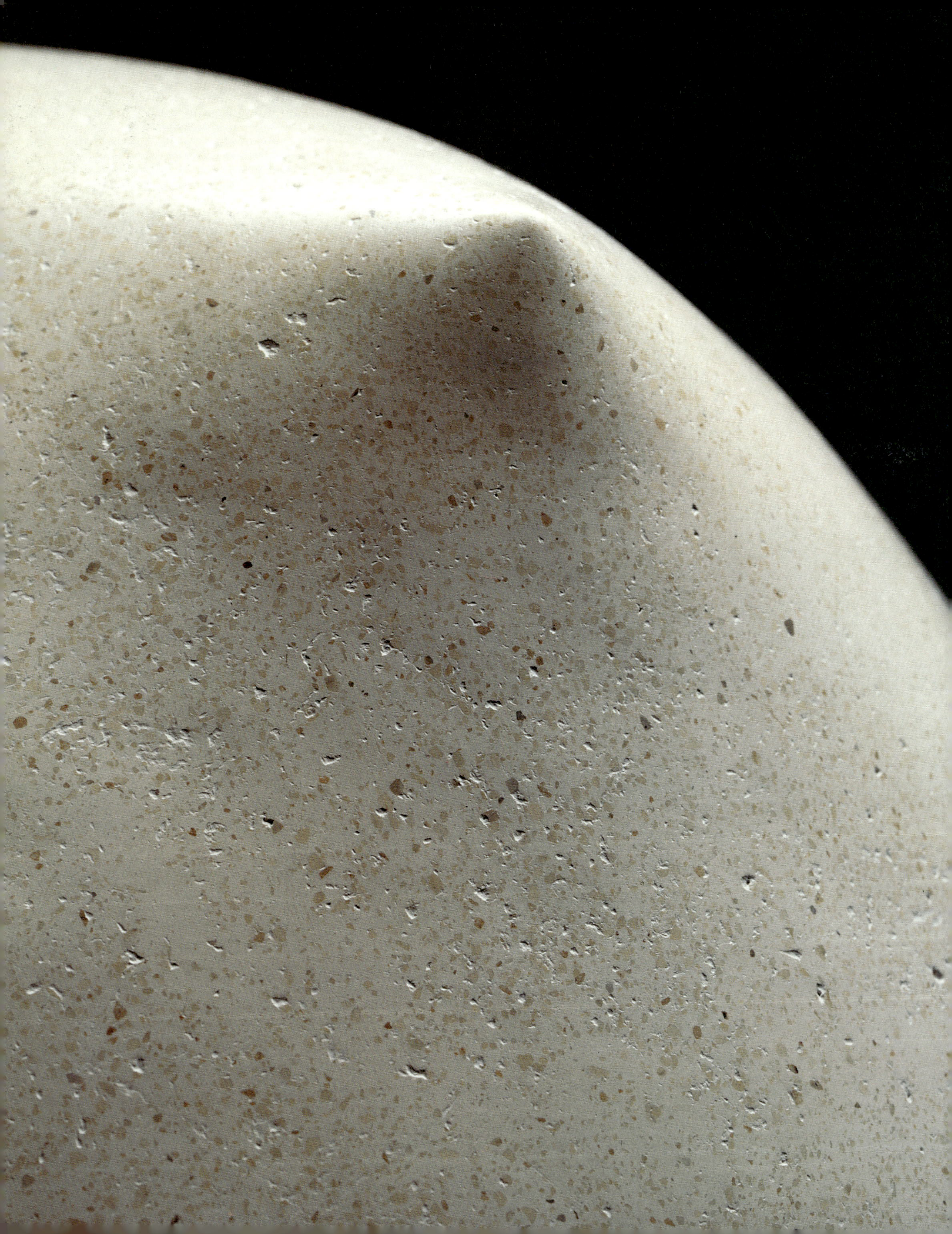

Sense
and
Perception

Felicity Aylieff

Manchester Art Gallery

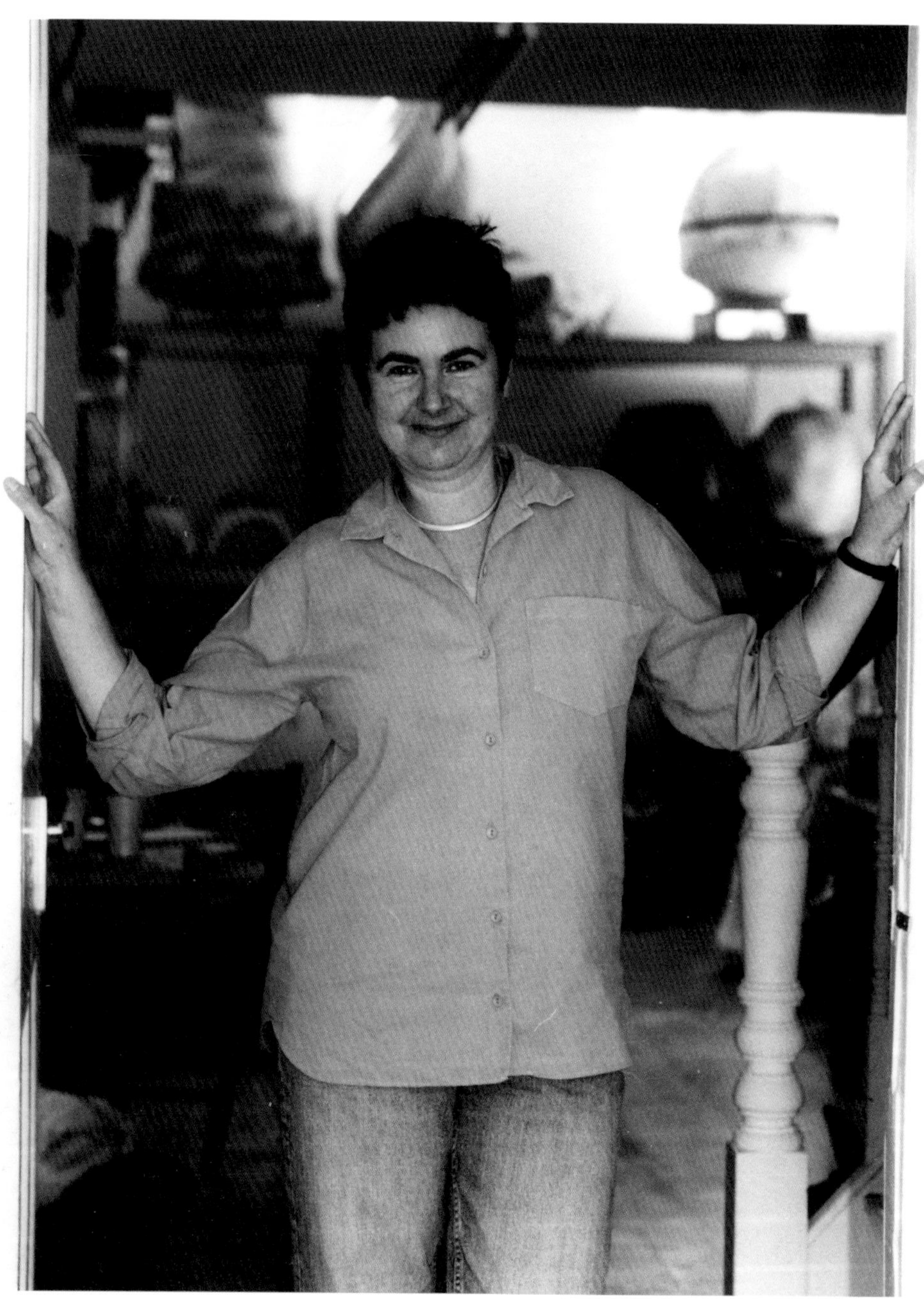

Felicity Aylieff in her studio

Foreword

Manchester Art Gallery is pleased to present *Sense and Perception,* an exhibition of ceramics by Felicity Aylieff. Aylieff's large scale abstract sculptures are extremely sensuous, exploiting the tactile qualities of clay to create intriguing, mysterious and seductive sculptural forms. They occupy an ambiguous space, somewhere between sculpture and ceramics.

This show comes at an important time for both the Gallery and the artist. Following our re-opening in May 2002, the Gallery has launched an ambitious and wide-ranging exhibitions programme in the new purpose-built galleries designed by Michael Hopkins & Partners. Aylieff's work has a particular affinity with this new space, her interest in form, mass and surface treatment are reflected in the proportions and materials of the architecture. Indeed, she has created a site-specific wall piece in response to the undulating rhythms of the massive concrete ceiling.

The exhibition marks a significant period in Aylieff's career, tracing the development of a body of work that began at the Royal College of Art in 1996. Since then she has established a growing reputation for sculptural forms in delicate textured and coloured clays, culminating in her nomination for the Jerwood Applied Arts Prize in 2001. This year she returned to the Royal College, in the role of Senior Tutor: Ceramics and Glass. It seems an appropriate point at which to pause and consider the direction her work has taken.

We would like to thank Manchester Metropolitan University and, in particular, Alex McErlain, Ceramics Lecturer, who first proposed the idea for this exhibition. He and Liz Mitchell, Curator (Decorative Art), have worked closely to bring the project to fruition, assisted by Natasha Howes, Curator (Exhibitions). The spirit of collaboration between our two institutions has been extremely beneficial, and we have no doubt it will lead to further collaborative projects.

We would like to thank Emma Maiden and Helen Bevis for their thoughtful and personal catalogue essays, and Richard Weltman and Steve Yates for their beautiful photography.

We are also grateful to the Arts Council of England for their support through the National Touring Programme.

Finally, and above all, we must thank Felicity Aylieff for working tirelessly, in the midst of a heavy teaching commitment, to create the content of this exhibition. She has been supported in this by the Royal College of Art, Bath Spa University College and her assistant Kelly Allsopp who has been extremely generous with her time and energy. Unusually, Aylieff has allowed us to make this a 'touch-friendly' show - visitors are invited to explore the works on display by hand as well as eye, providing an intimacy of experience that is not usually permitted in a public art gallery. It is an exciting and courageous prospect.

Virginia Tandy, Director
Howard Smith, Head of Curatorial Services
Manchester City Galleries

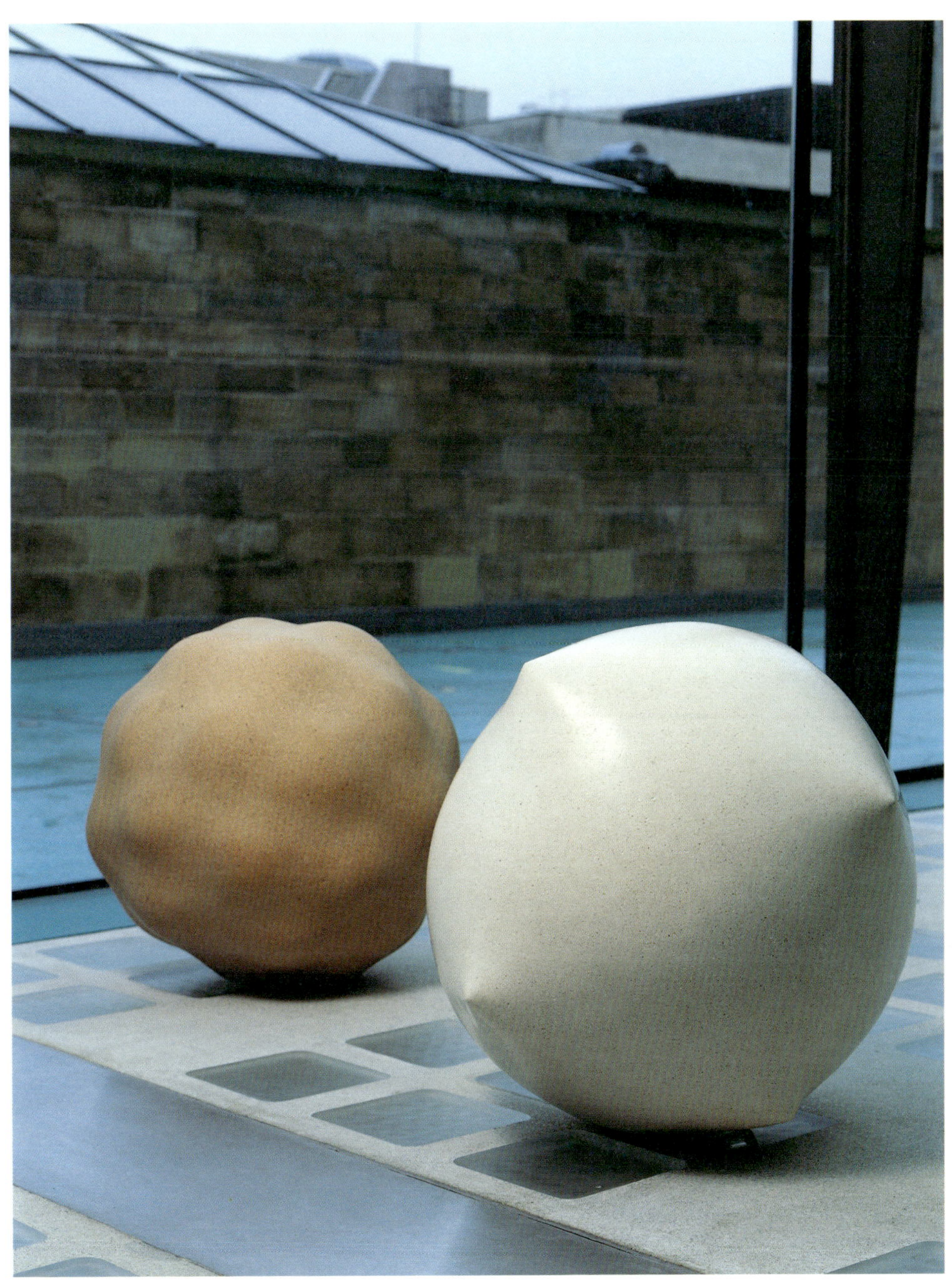

Bud and *Softly, Softly* 2001

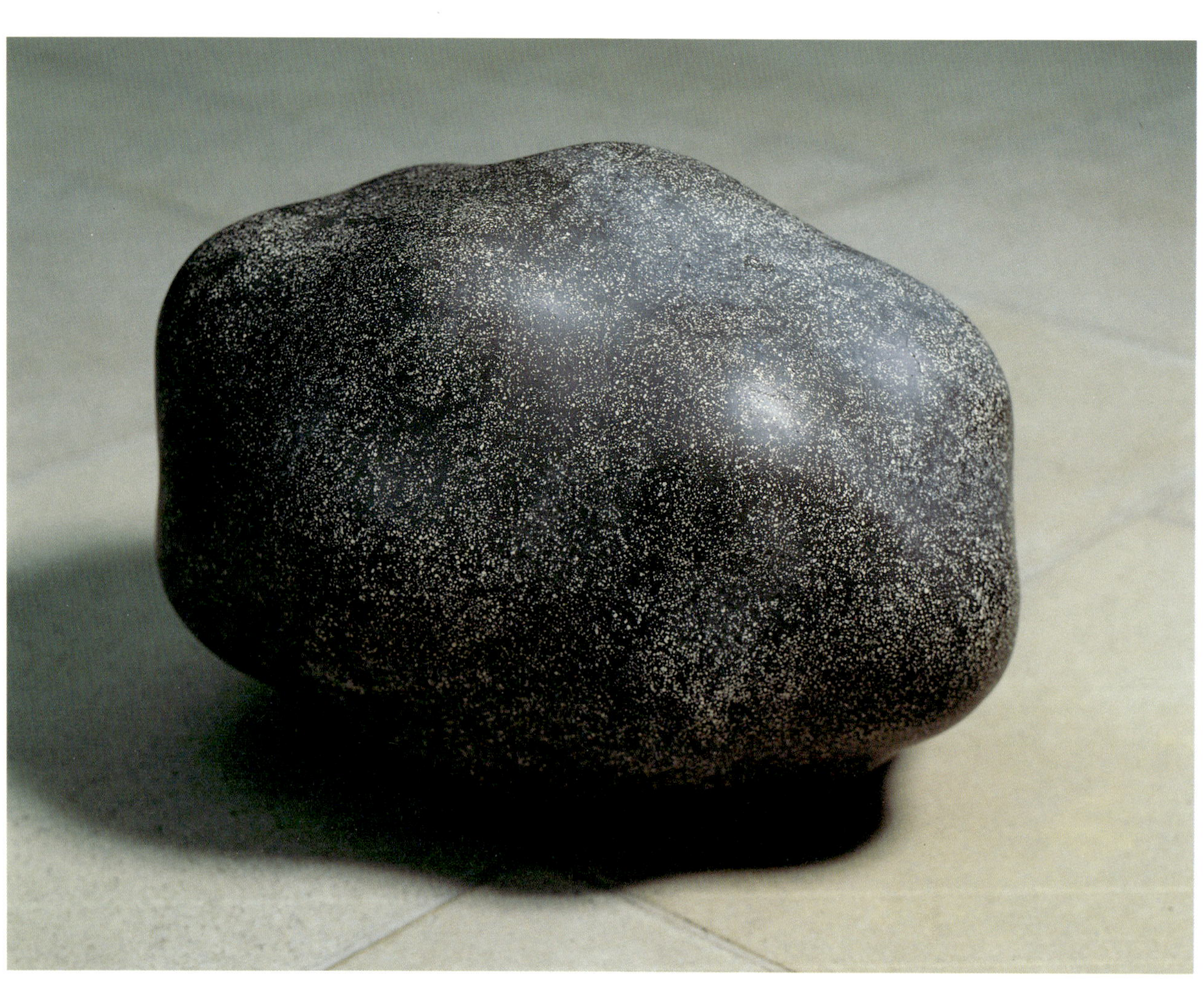

Black Cloud 2000

Felicity Aylieff
Emma Maiden

Felicity Aylieff is one of a number of contemporary ceramicists whose work crosses the boundaries of ceramics and sculpture, but she is one of very few who do it with ease. This major exhibition, Aylieff's first solo show in a public museum, presents her work in a context which allows a fresh appreciation of its sculptural concerns, and is particularly relevant at a time when the historical divisions between craft and art are fast dissolving.

These large clay pieces do not aim to be anything other than what they are: the result of an ongoing personal enquiry into material and form that Aylieff has pursued since her vessel-making beginnings, and although the work has moved into a more sculptural realm, its roots in pottery remain fundamental. The undulating silhouettes of her earlier hand-built ceramics are evident here in these gentle swells and rhythms. Volume, the space within the object - a pivotal concept in ceramics - has become even more important in these sculptures, to the extent that the void, paradoxically, is now the content.

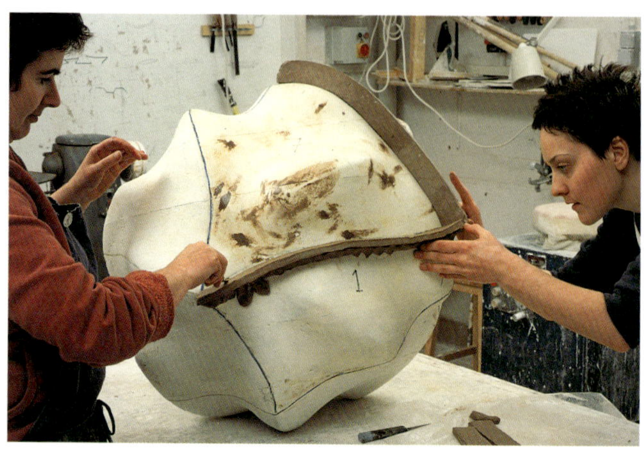

Fig 1

Mostly these volumes are completely enclosed. Hidden from view they are mysterious, unreachable, but they have an undeniable presence. For Aylieff the void is not inert and empty but is imbued with an energy that animates the external form from within. The clay, once fired, is rendered hard and stone-like, yet the soft bumps and waves that seem to ripple through it introduce a softness, a sense of it being a living membrane stretched and distorted by this vital inner force. In pieces such as *Soft Form* and *Softly, Softly* the quiet colours and subtle distension encourage a whole range of shadowy tones and highlights, so that the forms really do seem animated and light. The fact that they have no fixed base - unusual in ceramics but not in sculpture - suggests a variety of possible positions and invites the viewer to explore their full-bodied shapes from various angles. The eye travels across and around them, running along spirals or bouncing over ridges, discovering rhythm and contrast in taut, purposeful lines; appreciation of these forms becomes a dynamic experience in itself.

Aylieff makes work of a size rarely seen in ceramics. She always wanted to make large work, a desire frustrated at art college in the seventies, when domestic-scale functional ware was the general limit of ceramic aspiration. Returning to college in 1993, however, this time for an MPhil at the Royal College of Art, Aylieff at last had the time and space to explore ideas that had lain dormant for years. She could have carried on handbuilding and made the work larger, but that would have involved making the same forms, only scaled up. Instead, she wanted to investigate ideas about sculpture and form, to find out what these meant to her, and this involved a total revision of her materials and methods. At the RCA, with access to makers and resources from other disciplines, Aylieff made new discoveries. She started to carve shapes for mould making out of Styrofoam, used by the vehicle design department for modelling cars. It is unprepossessing stuff, lightweight like polystyrene, but easy to carve and because it is light and manoeuvrable Aylieff can work as large as her kiln allows.

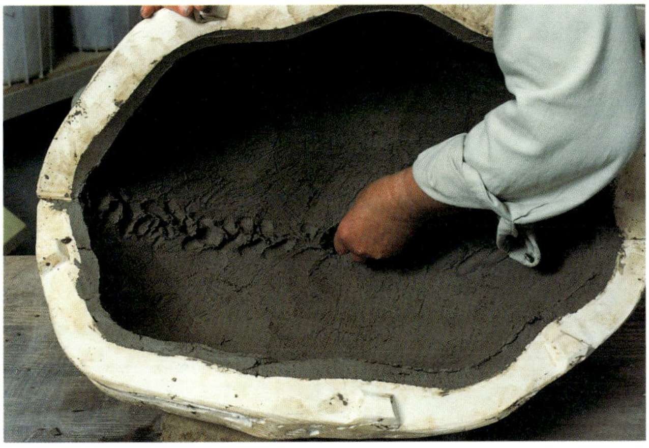

Fig 2

She glues the thick Styrofoam strips into a block and, with drawings and maquettes as reference, maps the design on the block, marking the high points as a stonemason would, then - less conventionally - carves into them with saw, electric knife and surform, eventually reaching the shapes that will be reproduced in clay. The next step is mould making in plaster, an exacting technique which may involve many sections that, fitted together, create the negative space into which the clay is pressed for the final sculpture.

It is an unusually industrial and complex process comprising elements from both ceramics and sculpture, and, because there are so many stages involved, it has to be underpinned by rigorous planning. Clay objects thrown on the wheel or built up by hand can be revised and altered during their making, but there is no such flexibility here. Aylieff's forms have to be fully resolved at the initial drawing and modelling stage. As drawings can only offer one view, she makes small clay maquettes that can be turned in the hand, allowing a consideration of the form from all angles. Roughly modelled, they are left raw and

unfired and are often discarded afterwards. After all they are only one step of the whole making process, not ends in themselves. And yet these little three-dimensional sketches are hugely important - they represent the only stage in what is largely a distanced method of production that is hands-on, intuitive, where there is a fluid interaction between material and idea; they are the original spark. The honed, finished shapes which emerge from the moulds at the other end of the making process are very different things indeed. Sanded, smoothed and polished, they are flawless, complete. But refined as they are, something of that spark inhabits them still. They have the life and spirit of those freely formed maquettes, and, strangely considering their size, the same quality of intimacy and warmth.

Aylieff spent much of her two-year research project at the RCA developing clay bodies that would withstand both the scale to which she was pushing her work and the rigours of construction and firing. The outcome of her research was a material she called 'ceramic terrazzo', a unique clay body containing pre-fired fragments of coloured clay and glass.

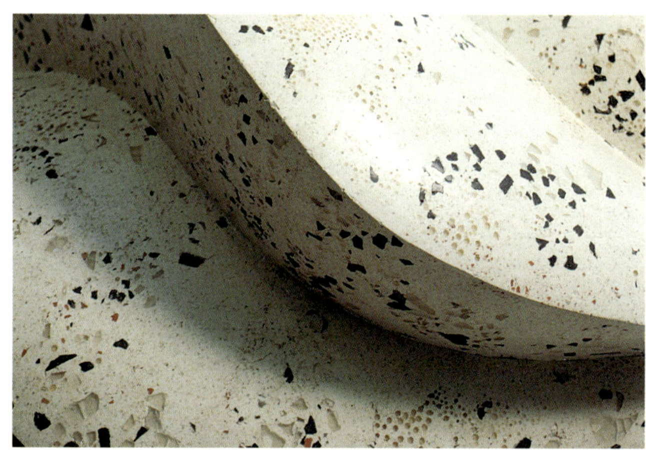

Fig 3

Once fired, it can be ground and polished with machines which cut through these particles, resulting in a smooth surface embedded with random patterns of colour. As well as adding visual richness and interest, the pre-fired materials also strengthen the clay and allow it to dry without cracking, essential for making work on this scale.

When it comes to surface, Aylieff eschews the conventional ceramic coverings of slips and glazes, preferring instead to exploit the aesthetic and tactile qualities of the clay itself. Colour and texture are integral to the form rather than sitting on the surface as a glaze would. Terrazzo was well suited to the large, regular, more symmetrical forms Aylieff was making at the Royal College, but in recent years, as her ideas and points of reference have changed, so her material has had to change. Softer forms demanded a subtler effect, and Aylieff developed a white clay body to which she could add fine grog, or pre-fired clay, for strength, and special stains to achieve the required depth of colour. The glassy hardness of terrazzo that enhanced the crisp, carved quality of earlier pieces has given way to gentler effects that suit the more subtle forms.

For Aylieff, material and idea must always work hand in hand. And ideas are constantly evolving. Many of the terrazzo pieces made at the Royal College were inspired by objects, particularly the twelfth century Indian carvings, found in the British Museum. The natural world, too, was a rich source of shape and pattern. But more recently Aylieff has begun to move away from recognisable imagery and into a more abstract sphere, with the aim of creating forms that have a stronger emotional resonance. They retain much of the rhythm and movement of previous work, yet because they rely on a personal, intuitive sense of form rather than an external iconography they have an independence and particularity that sets them apart. They also seem more fluid. Forms are defined, but somehow not finalised. It is as if the energy inside might push them further, as if they are still growing, still becoming.

This same spirit of openness led Aylieff to make certain site-specific pieces for this show. She responded strongly to the new extension at Manchester Art Gallery, particularly to Hopkins' use of materials such as concrete and oak, whose qualities of colour and texture resonate with her own work.

The exhibition space, too, echoes her own concern with enclosed interiors - there are no windows - and with form, inspiring the wall piece *Code* whose shape corresponds to the arches in the ceiling construction.

Manchester Art Gallery is unusual amongst museums in having an exhibitions programme that does not make hierarchical distinctions between decorative and fine art, making it an ideal context for art such as Aylieff's that resists traditional definitions. Born out of an intensive exploration of ideas and materials, Aylieff's work has a strong sense of its own existence. She has forged her own unique sculptural language and her forms, having evolved through time, possess their own logic and, above all, integrity. This exhibition marks an important stage in Aylieff's career and enables exciting new work that might normally be confined to smaller, specialist galleries, to be accessed by a wider public.

Fig 1 Placing clay collars around a styrofoam model

Fig 2 Pressing clay into the plaster mould

Fig 3 *Projection* 1996

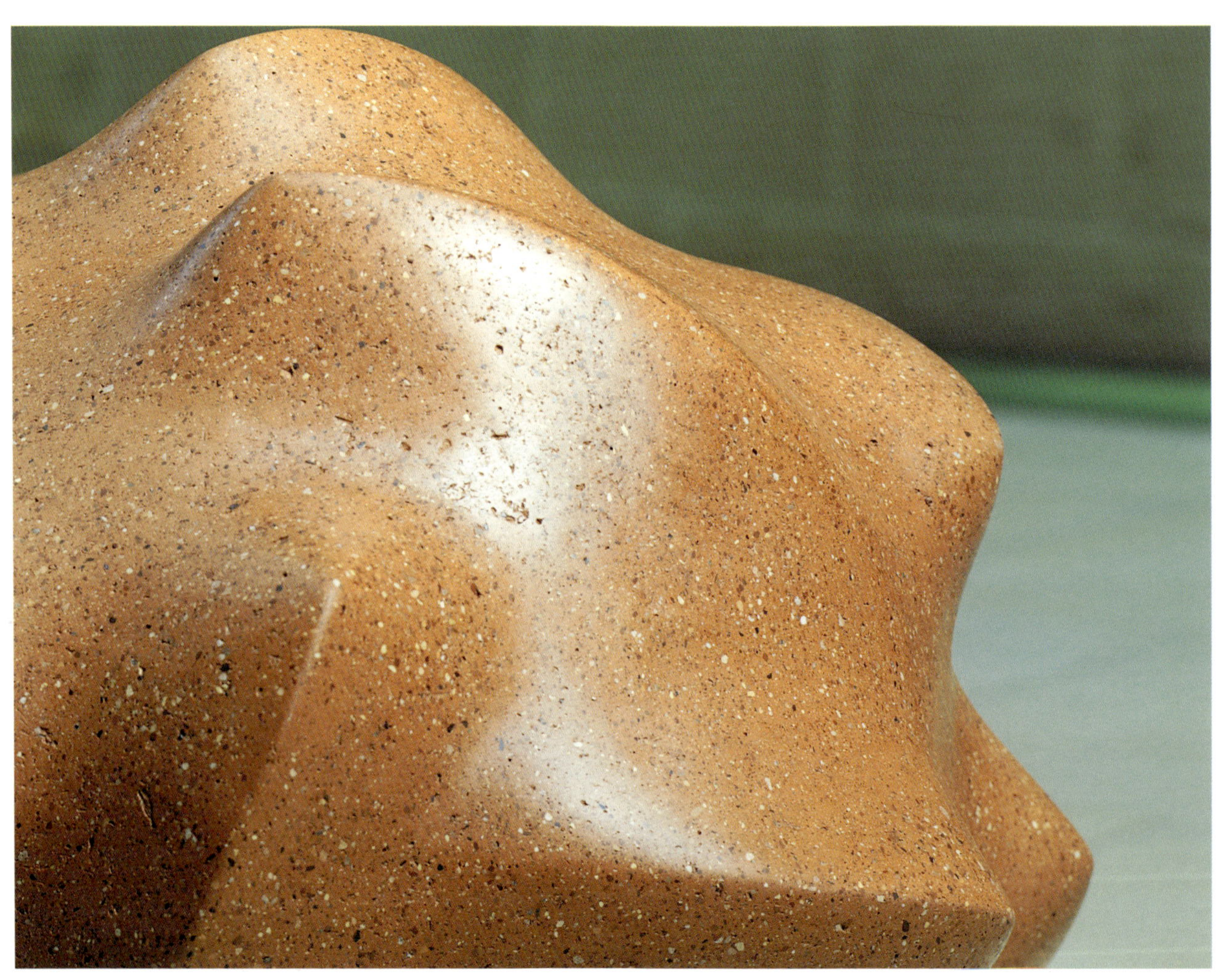

Bittersweet (detail) 2001

Perceptive Touch
Helen Bevis

Curators have a dilemma. One of the perks of the job is to handle the objects in their care. They experience the object intimately, feeling the hidden, unfinished surfaces that reveal so much more than the fine finished exterior. In the quest for pieces to exhibit, curators handle, explore and consider each object, stroking surfaces to feel each embellishment, planned or accidental. If they dare they will do this without the omnipresent white curatorial glove: unsheathed hands find each mark left by the artist. Touch - surely the most intimate sense. And yet, the pieces will then go onto a white plinth, labelled, secured from risk and lit to perfection.

An object in a museum...must suffer the de-natured existence of an animal in a zoo...the object dies - of suffocation and the public gaze - whereas private ownership confers on the owner the right and the need to touch. As a young child will reach out to handle the thing it names, so the passionate collector, his eye in harmony with his hand, restores to the object the life giving touch of its maker.

Bruce Chatwin, Utz, Picador, 1988

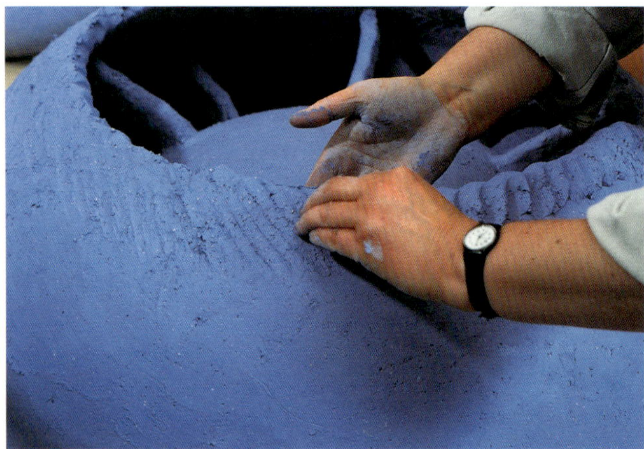

Fig 4

Displayed out of reach of our prying hands, we rely on sight alone to interpret the work, to tell us how surface relates to form. In *Sense and Perception*, however, Manchester Art Gallery is taking the unusual stance of discarding the 'Do Not Touch' signs. Felicity Aylieff's sculpture is there to be experienced at first hand, scrutinised at close quarters, even to be touched. Tactile information complements visual detail, we can discover for ourselves if they feel as sensual as they look. Aylieff's sculptural mastery of material and form, of senses and perception, is unveiled to all.

Clay - this primordial, therapeutic, malleable material, endlessly versatile yet often trapped by limited perceptions. It is a material associated with intimacy and touch, with objects made for handling. Hold a handmade pot and feel the spiralling lines formed while it is shaped by the potter's hands. Your hands become joined with theirs. Search for the identifying finger print of the potter, permanently baked into the surface - more personal than any signature.

This contact with the potter transcends time; even the earliest shards can reveal the whorls and indents of the maker's fingers. The sensuality of touch, the caress of the maker, is timeless.

Felicity Aylieff works in clay because it gives her the qualities of form and surface few other materials could. Throughout the complex making process of moulding, firing and finishing, the clay works with her, towards her sculptures. It doesn't fight the form. Technically and aesthetically her work is exacting, and far removed from the simplicity of throwing a pot on a wheel. It comes from a very personal exploration of form and surface. Her new body of work is part of a continual quest to bring together emotional and intellectual qualities of abstract form. Each piece is directed at heightening the senses, inviting us to question what we are seeing, touching and thinking. The function of the form is to stimulate.

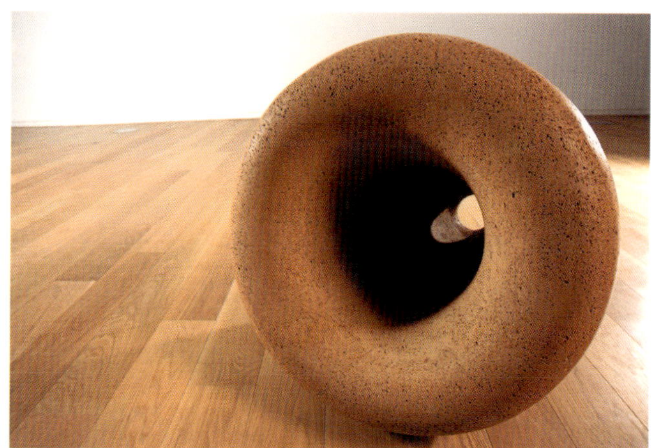
Fig 5

Colour further transforms our sense of the object. Preconceived notions of colour help us work our way around the world: clay is brown, the sky is blue and the sun is yellow. These are simplistic but effective guidelines to the colours that shape us. When they vary, we have to consider more deeply what we are looking at. The warm terracotta red of freshly dug clay is rich enough to let the clay be itself, no more and no less. Terracotta reds reinforce the naturalness of organic forms. Aylieff's earlier experiments with manufactured reds she felt argued with the forms. They encouraged perceptions of an otherness that stood apart from the sensation she was searching for. The colour seemed to overpower the form.

By contrast, Aylieff finds the colour blue responds to something intuitive in her. The rich eye-warming ethereal blues she uses are akin to *hoovooloo* blue - Douglas Adams' hyper intelligent shade. This is a blue that can think for itself, a blue that takes us into its depths: an oxymoronic warm-blue. In Aylieff's work it feels at home, an intrinsic part of the object, though far from the original colour of clay. It is an addition that feels like it has always belonged there, enhancing the qualities of the abstract shapes. Sculptures in opposites of black and white repel and attract each other. Both hues are strong, but one absorbs light and one reflects it. One sucks it in, drawing attention to the ripples and nuances of form, whilst the other throws it back, pushing the form into the surrounding space.

The language of the vessel is anthropomorphic. We talk of its mouth, neck, belly and foot. But then, our senses are always seeking to rationalise and compartmentalise the world around us. If we can identify recognisable shapes, the world is less threatening. Organic forms appeal to our rationalising view. The sense of the organic underlies much of Aylieff's work, though both in scale and surface quality we are far removed from the familiar. Her work is 'life-size' - its relationship with human scale and volume are part of its humanistic qualities, they help us relate to it. Too small and these objects become ornamental, too large and they could become oppressive. Their size is perfect.

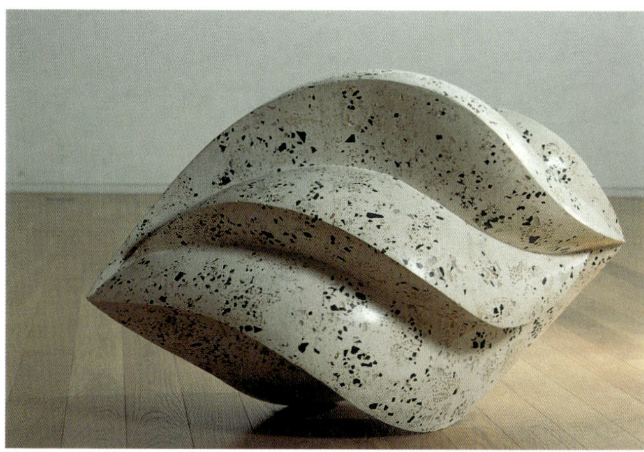

Fig 6

Seamless undulates about its internal space with an unstoppable profile. It gives the illusion of space, a single undulating line defining the space held within and the space outside in a single continuous movement. It seems perfectly self-contained. Whereas *Softly, Softly* is like the baby in the womb, kicking and pushing its way into the world, even before its time. It is greedy to inhabit the space around it. *Code* comprises a series of tall, slender pillar-like forms, made in response to the clean, uncluttered new space at Manchester Art Gallery. These totemic forms with their powerful sense of rhythm convey suggestions of sound, as the tall body sized cylinders seem to absorb the white noise around them and quietly reverberate to their inner energy. Just as the Easter Island figures hold their space and need no embellishment of speech, they speak through their presence. Perhaps then it is possible to hear a shape, in the sense that one hears its silence, hears the space it fills.

Sculpture can be viewed in many ways. First there is the pleasure of the two-dimensional profile it presents when first seen. But, for me, the exciting part happens as you move around it; three dimensions open up to be explored with your eyes and hands. Your senses demand answers from your brain. Does it really appear to float, sit or sink? Does it push into the space around it or does the space absorb its form? Each of us has our own perception.

Our intellectual sense of the material helps shape our perception of Aylieff's sculptures. Clay is not normally associated with sculpture of this scale. The very qualities of the material that make it perfect for her work seem to humble it in the eyes of the traditional art world. Aylieff's art is as much about the qualities of her chosen material as it is about the formal consideration of sculpture. Yet, her work leaps well beyond the confines of functional and conceptual ceramics. Decorative qualities still interest her but this work moves beyond the decorative, it is more subtle, more organic and more derived from her deep affinity with the material.

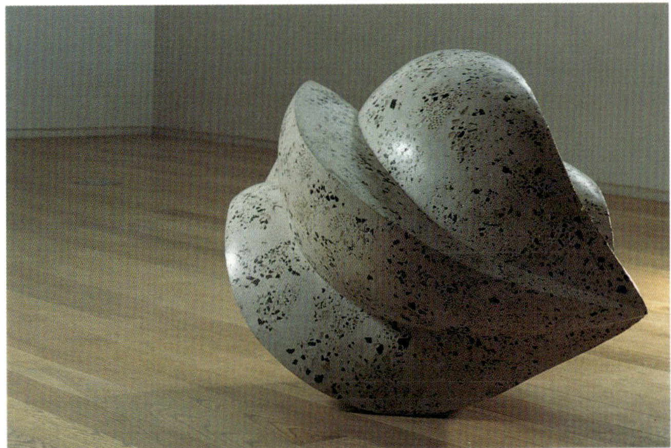

Fig 7

She works as a sculptor but in clay. Does that make her a potter? Our perception of the material is absolutely challenged by her work.

The perception of what these pieces are - art or craft - is confusingly relevant and irrelevant to what they mean. Does it matter? As sculpture they sit happily within the white space of a gallery, as craft objects they could seem like pretenders to the art-throne. Somehow, the category in which we place these objects shapes how we see them. *Sense and Perception* is an exhibition to kick us into thinking about what we are seeing or perceiving. Are we looking at big pots or small sculptures? The curatorial dilemma is resolved if we have the freedom to let our senses work this out for ourselves.

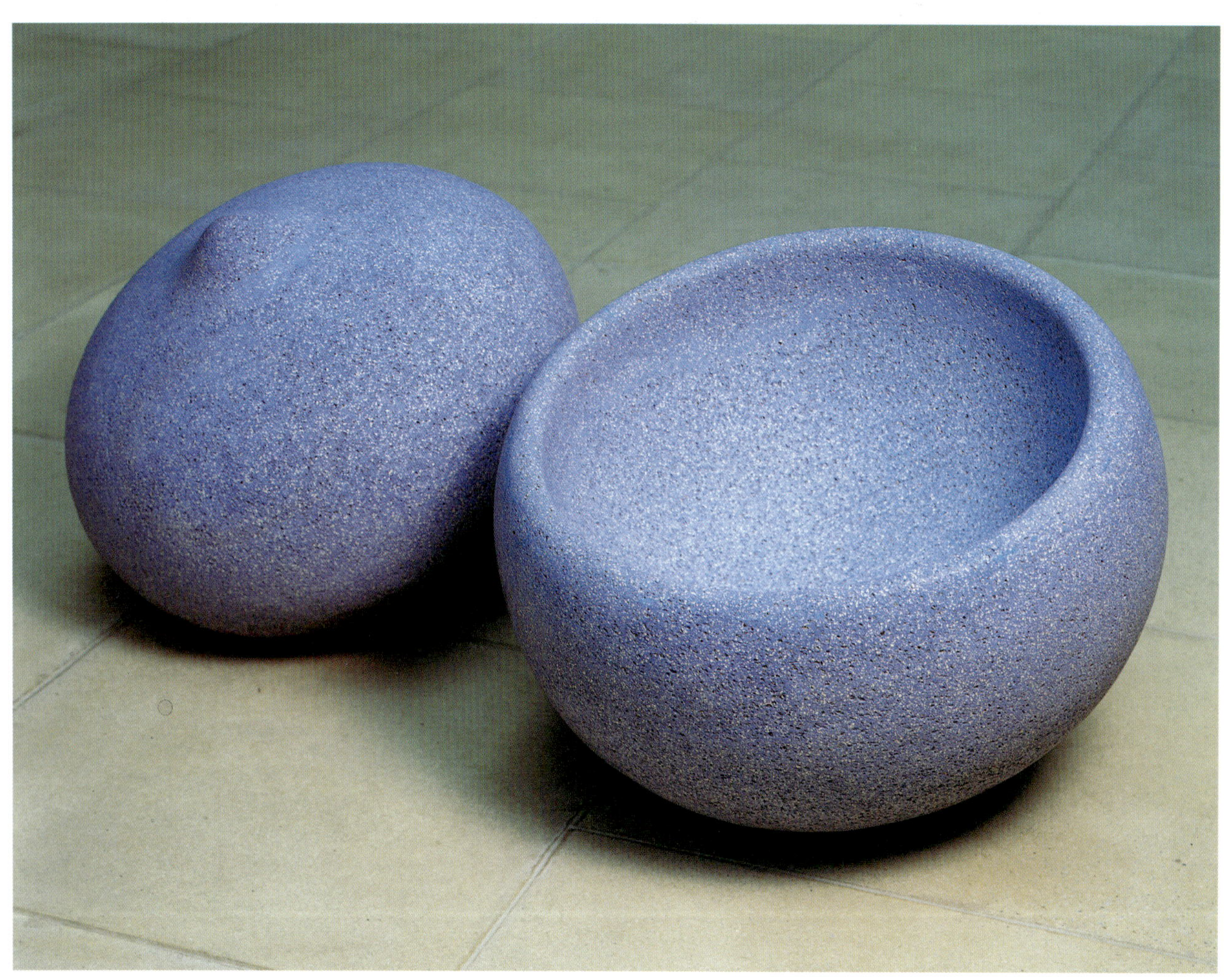

Misfit 2001

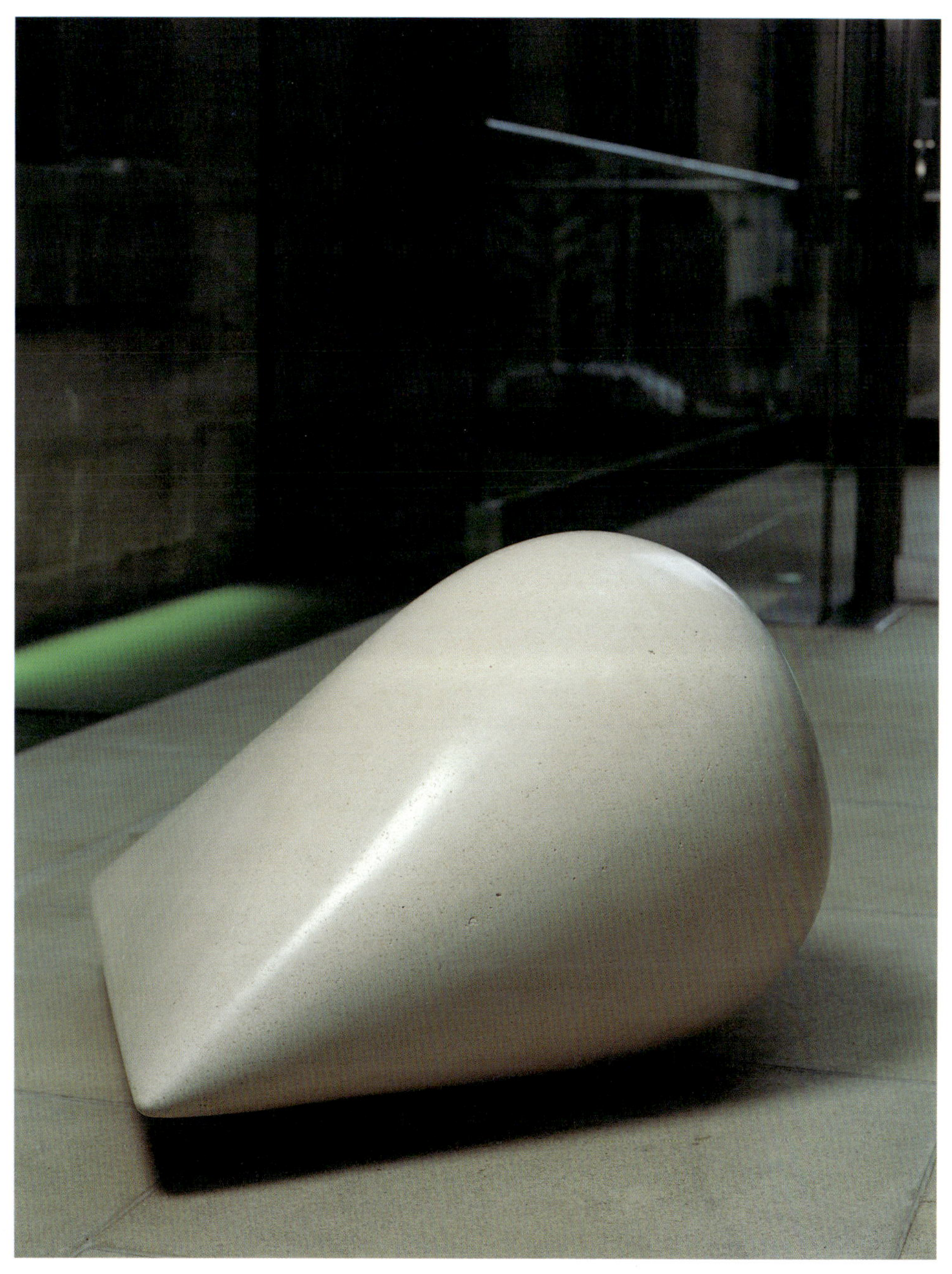

Thin End 2002

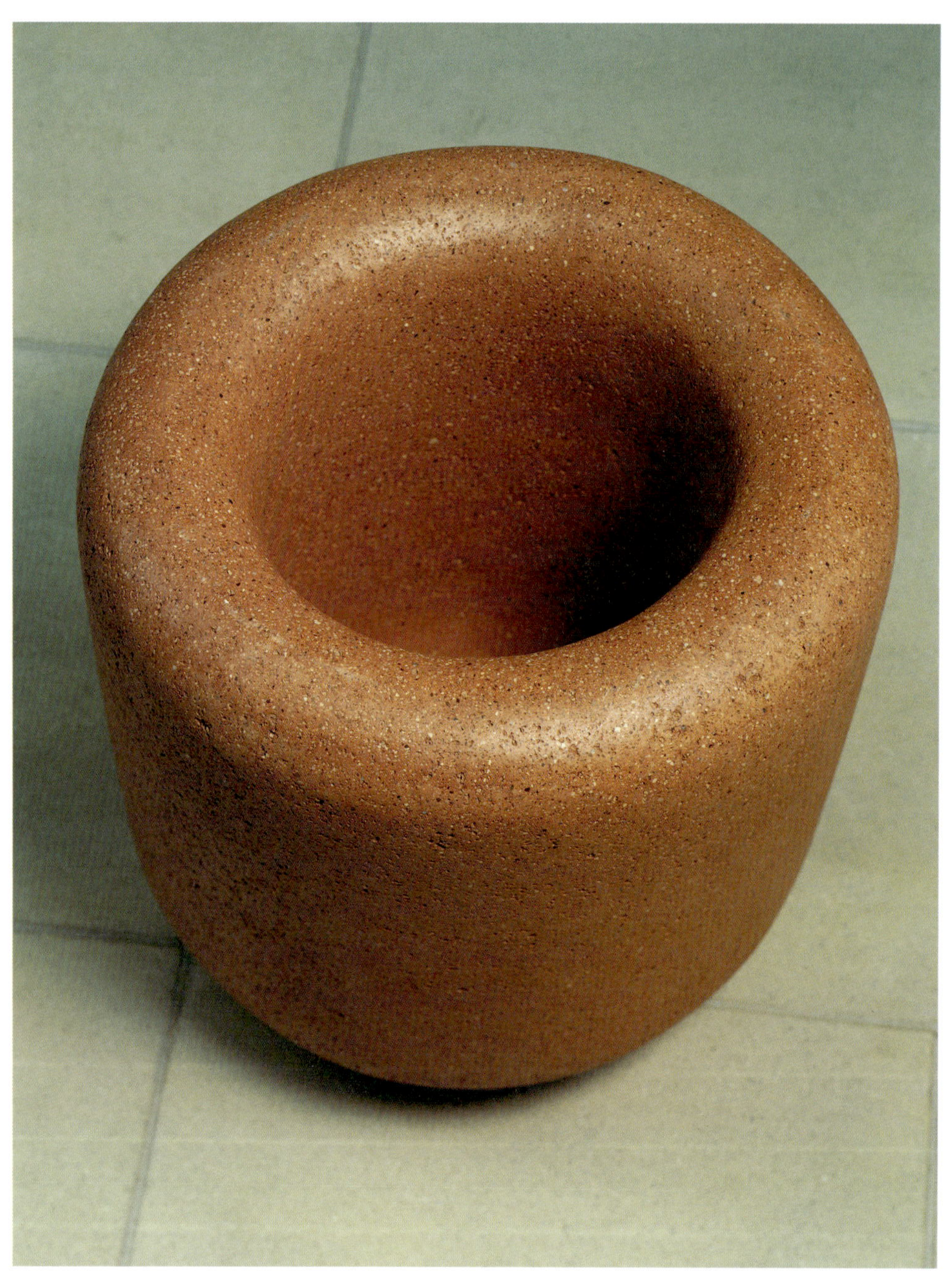

Seamless-Red 2002

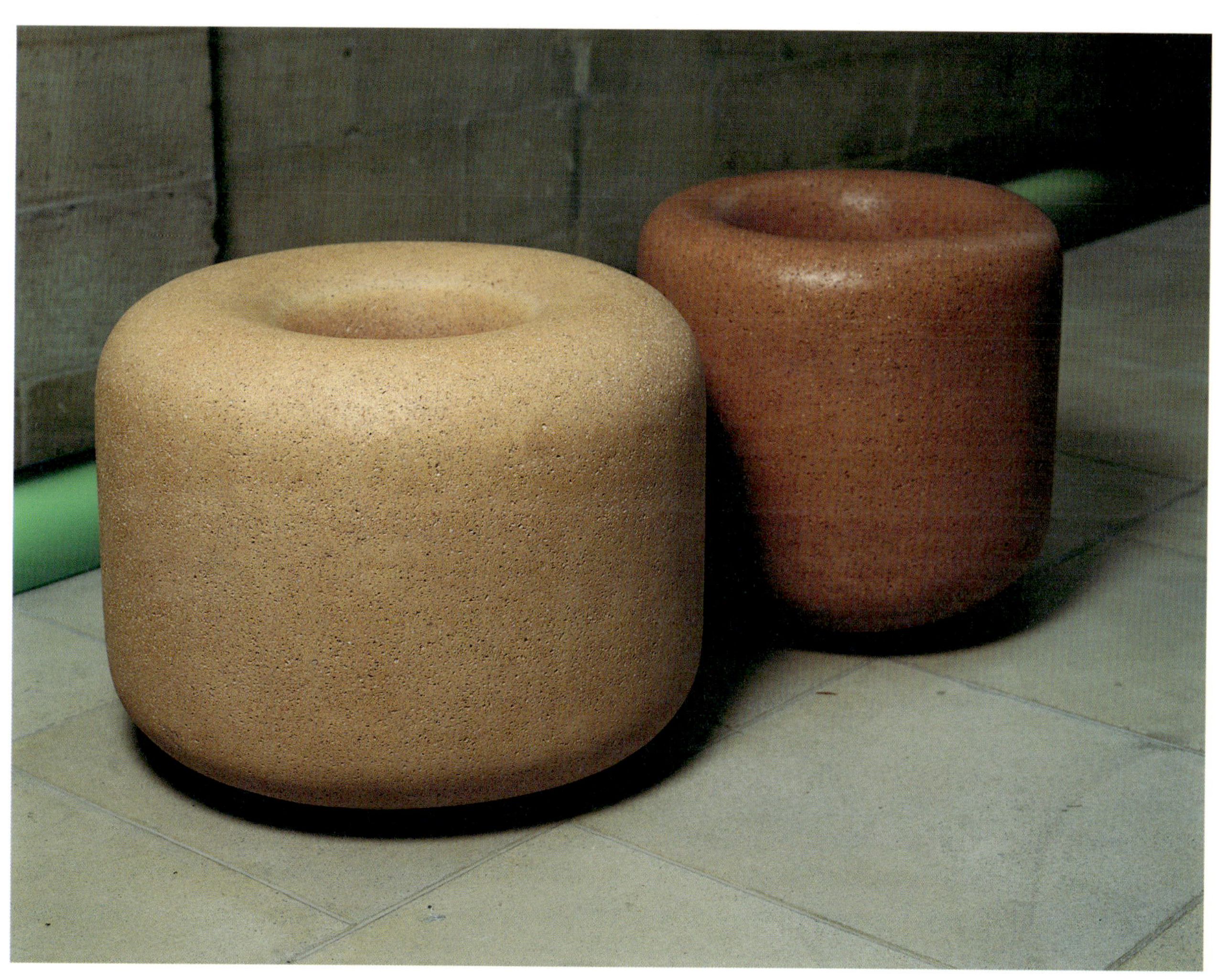

Seamless - Gold and *Seamless - Red* 2002

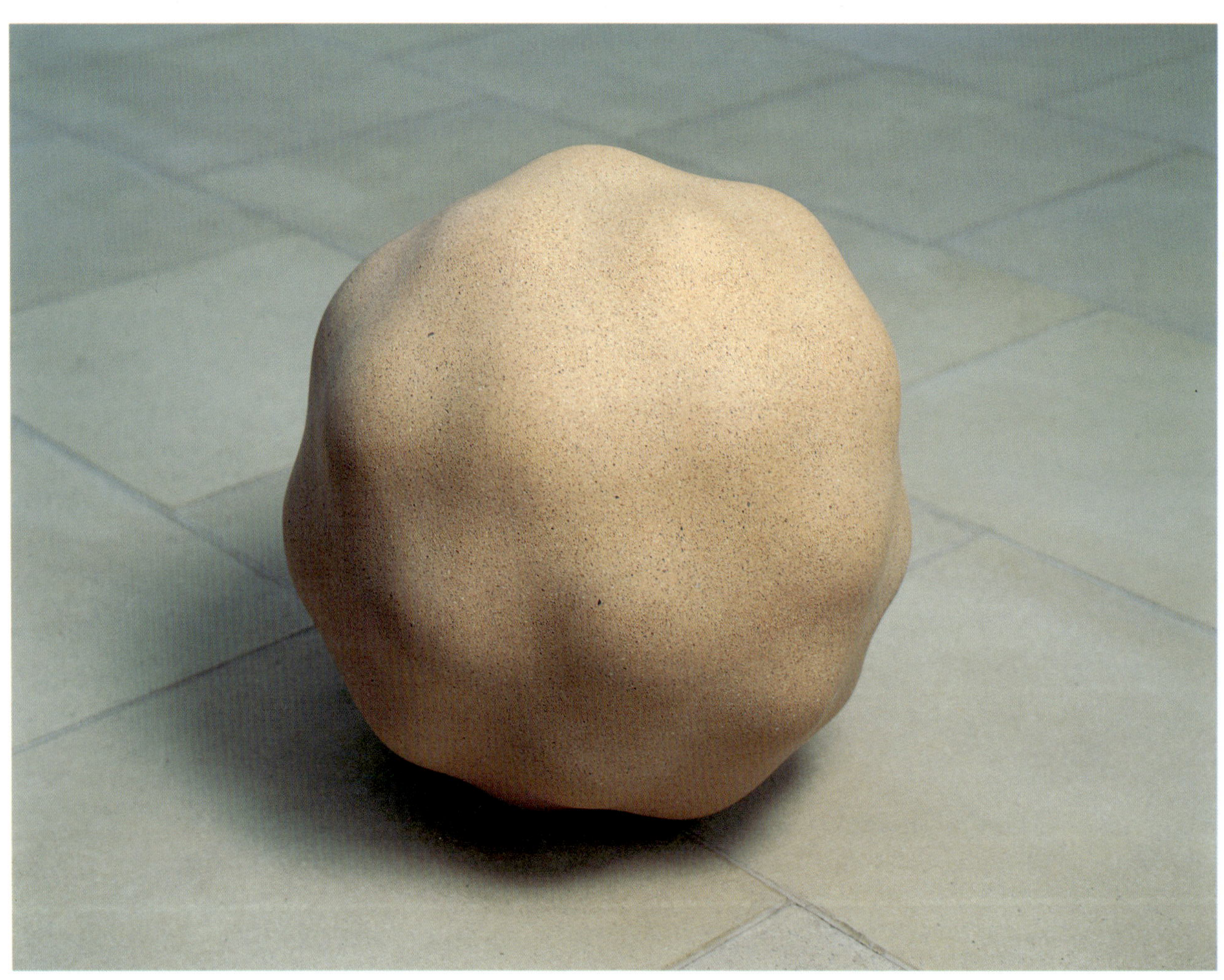

Softly, Softly 2001

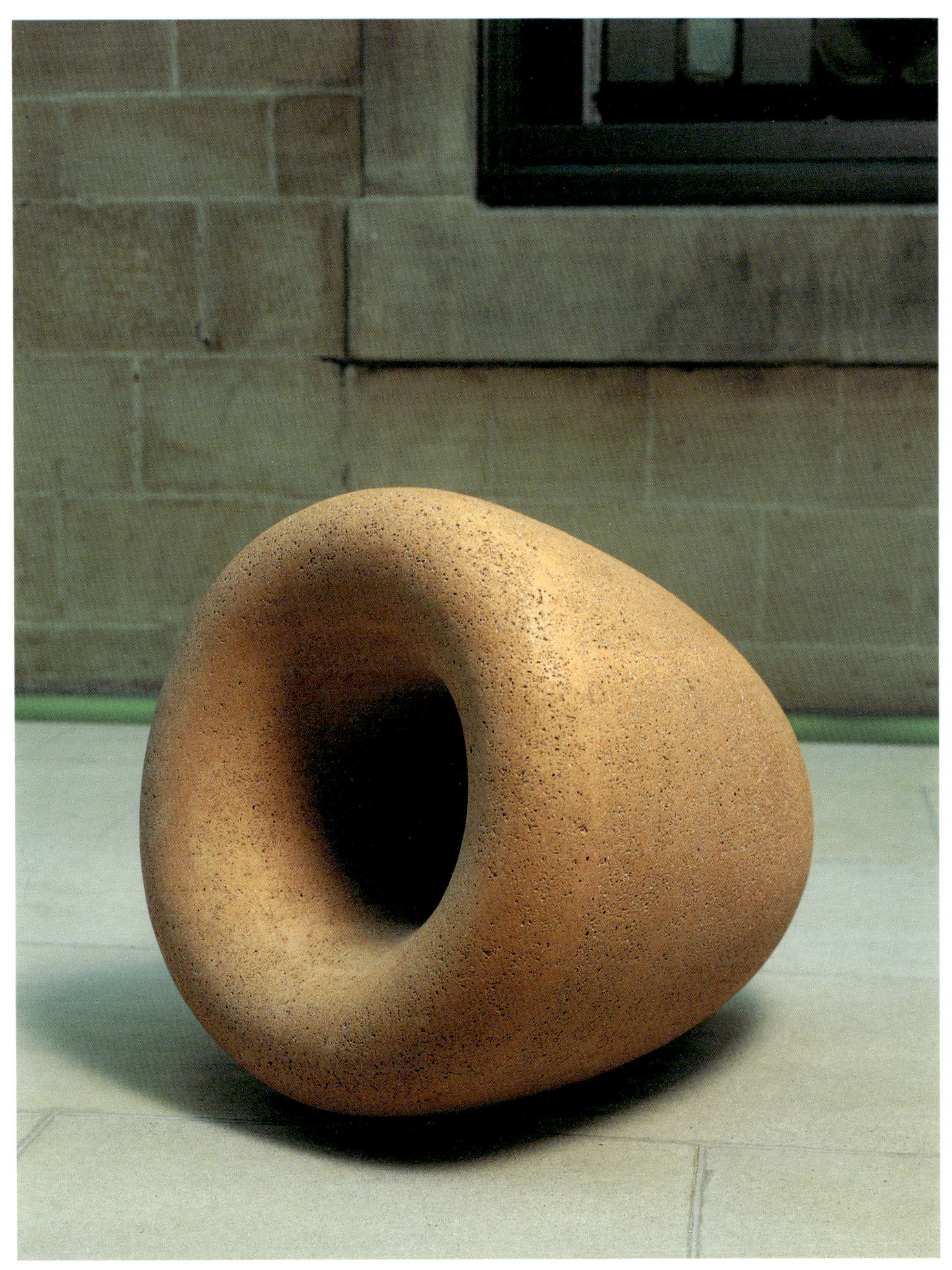

Echo 2001

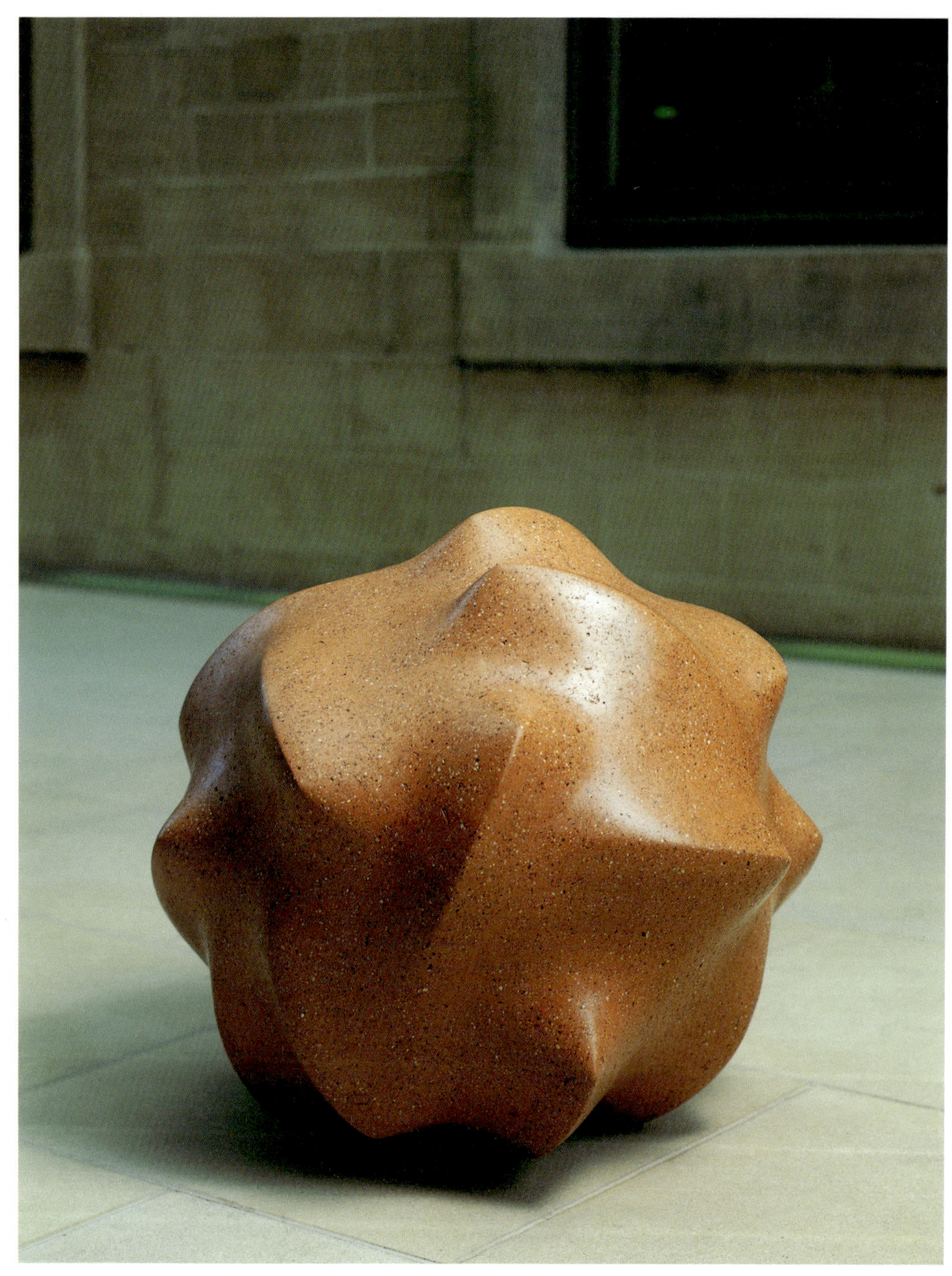

Bittersweet 2001

List of works

This list details all the work selected for exhibition.
However, works on display may vary at each venue depending on the space available.
Dimensions are given in centimetres, height x width x depth.

1. *Twist and Turn* 1996 — Press moulded white clay body, with aggregates of fired coloured porcelain, fired terracotta and borosilicate and ballotini glass
114 x 70 x 75

2. *Projection* 1996 — Hand formed white clay body, with aggregates of fired coloured porcelain, fired terracotta and borosilicate and ballotini glass
60 x 80 x 110

3. *Blue Cloud* 2000 — Press moulded blue clay body, with aggregates of fired coloured porcelain
49 x 35 x 35

4. *Black Cloud* 2000 — Press moulded black clay body, with aggregates of fired coloured porcelain
49 x 35 x 35

5. *Bittersweet* 2001 — Press moulded Almondsbury red brick clay
54 x 56 x 56

6. *Softly, Softly* 2001 — Press moulded Almondsbury gold brick clay
56 x 56 x 56

7. *Bud* 2001 — Press moulded white clay body, with aggregates of fired porcelain
56 x 56 x 56

8. *Echo* 2001 — Hand formed aerated Almondsbury gold brick clay
56 x 56 x 65

9. *Misfit* 2001 — Hand formed aerated blue clay body, with aggregates of fired coloured porcelain
Bowl: 35 x 58 x 58, Ball: 35 x 58 x 58

10. *Thin End* 2002

Press moulded white clay body,
with aggregates of fired coloured
porcelain
50 x 70 x 70

11. *Seamless-Red* 2002

Hand formed Almondsbury red
brick clay
54 x 46 x 46

12. *Seamless-Gold* 2002

Hand formed Almondsbury gold
brick clay
54 x 54 x 54

13. *Passage* 2002

Hand formed white clay body, with
aggregates of fired porcelain
54 x 70 x 70

14. *One Way
    or Another* 2002

Press moulded white clay body,
with aggregates of fired
porcelain.
Press moulded black clay body,
with aggregates of fired
porcelain
Each piece: 60 x 72 x 72

15. *Tall Order* 2002

Press moulded Almondsbury red
brick clay 130 x 40 x 40

16. *Cubed Sphere* 2002

Press moulded white clay body,
with aggregates of fired
porcelain
70 x 70 x 70

17. *Code* 2002

Press moulded white paper clay
body, with aggregates of fired
porcelain
Five pillars, each 130 x 25 x 25

Artist's Biography

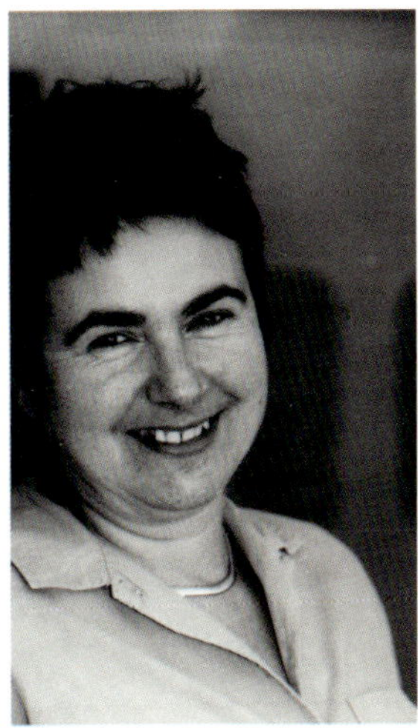

1954   Born in Bedfordshire

Education and Training
1975-77   Bath Academy of Art
          BA (Hons) Ceramics

1993-96   Royal College of Art
          MPhil Postgraduate Research: Ceramics

Teaching
1978-82   Bedales School, Hampshire
          Ceramics, General Art and Design

1982-89   Bath College of Higher Education
          Associate Lecturer, Foundation, Adult Studies
          Lecturer, BA (Hons) Ceramics

1987 on   Visiting tutor to Cardiff, Glasgow, Falmouth,
          Limerick, Loughborough

          External examiner to Wolverhampton
          School of Art & Design

1989-2001 Bath Spa University
          Lecturer, BA (Hons) Ceramics
          Awarded Professorship 2001

2002   Royal College of Art
          Senior Tutor: Ceramics and Glass

Solo Exhibitions
1996   *Felicity Aylieff - The Elusive Body*
          Victoria Art Gallery, Bath

1997   *Felicity Aylieff*
          Goed Werk GCV Centre for Spacial and Graphic
          Design, Zulte, Belgium

1998   *Dashed, Speckled, Brushed*
          Loes and Reinier, International Ceramics, Deventer,
          Netherlands

1999   *Sculpture and Pots*
          Bedales Gallery, Petersfield, Hants

2000   *Felicity Aylieff, new work, an evolution*
          The Scottish Gallery, Edinburgh

2001   *Felicity Aylieff*
          Galerie Marianne Heller, Heidelberg, Germany

Selected Group Exhibitions
1996   *Contemporary Crafts in Avon*
          Bristol Museum and Art Gallery

          Gestaltendes Handwerk
          Munich International Trade Fair, Germany

          British Ceramics
          Keramik Galerie - Hilde Holdestein, Bremen, Germany

1997   *Summer Exhibition*
          Hannah Peschar Gallery and Sculpture Garden, Surrey

          Fletcher Challenge Ceramic Award
          Auckland Museum, Auckland, New Zealand

          Ceramists of Fame and Promise
          Beaux Arts Gallery, Bath

          Summer in the Garden
          Contemporary Applied Arts, London

          Slip, Crackle, Pot
          Six Chapel Row, Bath

1998   *International Group Exhibition*
          Global Ceramics, Babel, Amsterdam, Netherlands

          Quite White
          Brewery Arts, Cirencester

          Young British Sculptors
          Beaux Arts Gallery, Bath

Contemporary Sculpture
Roche Court Sculpture Garden, Surrey

Women in Europe
Galerie Marianne Heller, Heidelberg, Germany

1999   *Ceramic Contemporaries 3*
Crafts Council, London and touring

*International Competition & Exhibition:
Westerwald prize*
Keramikmuseum, Westerwald, Germany

Ceramiques Britannique Contemporaines
Bandol France, Galerie Hamelin, Honfleur, France

Garden of Delight
Ceramic Millennium, Vlaardingen, Netherlands

Not Just Pots
Southern Arts and Hampshire Museum Services
touring exhibition

2000   *Insideout*
Flow, London

Sensuous Proposals
Contemporary Applied Art, London

New Directions in Sculpture
Glynn Vivian Art Gallery, Swansea

International Group Exhibition
Lucerne 2000 Ceramic Biennale, Switzerland

Still Form, Bright Line
Canary Wharf, London

Paper Clay Plus
Crawford Arts Centre, St Andrews, Scotland

2001   *Sculpture in a Scottish Garden*, Edinburgh

*British Studio Ceramics: Works from the New
Millennium*
The Clay Studio, Philadelphia, USA

World Ceramic Biennale, 2001, Korea

Great Britain
Terra Keramiek, Delft, Netherlands

Jerwood Applied Arts Prize: Ceramics
Crafts Council, London and touring

SOFA
Chicago, USA

Awards

1999   Shortlisted for the Westerwald prize for
Ceramic Sculpture, Germany

2001   Shortlisted for the Jerwood Applied Arts
Prize: Ceramics

2001   Diploma of Honor, World Ceramic Biennale, Korea

Commissions/Collections

1997   Auckland Museum, New Zealand

1998   Hessisches Landesmuseum, Darmstadt, Germany

1999   Prior's Court School, Woodland sculpture,
Berkshire
Keramikmuseum, Westerwald, Germany

2000   Victoria & Albert Museum

2001   World Ceramic Centre, Korea

Work represented by

Hannah Peschar Sculpture Garden, Surrey
Roche Court Sculpture Park, Salisbury
Adrian Sassoon, London
Nancy Margolis, New York

Membership

Crafts Council Index of Selected Makers
Contemporary Applied Arts
Fellow of the Craft Potters Association

Authored reviews and articles

Numerous articles, exhibitions and book reviews including

'Larger than Life' Felicity Aylieff
'Ceramic Review' No.165

'Space Odyssey' Martin Smith
Ceramic Review No.176

'Basic Form' Takeshi Yasuda
Ceramic Review No.180

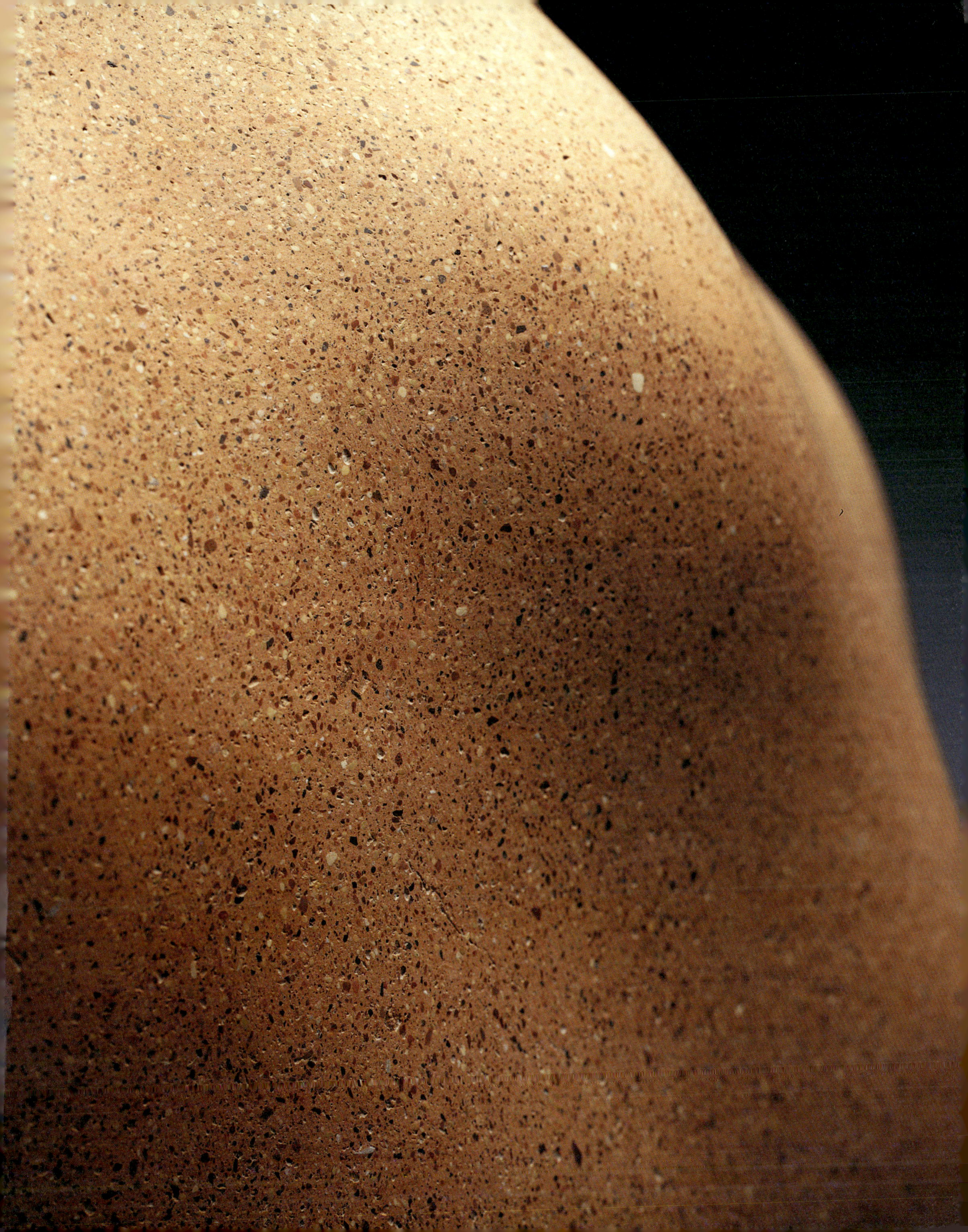

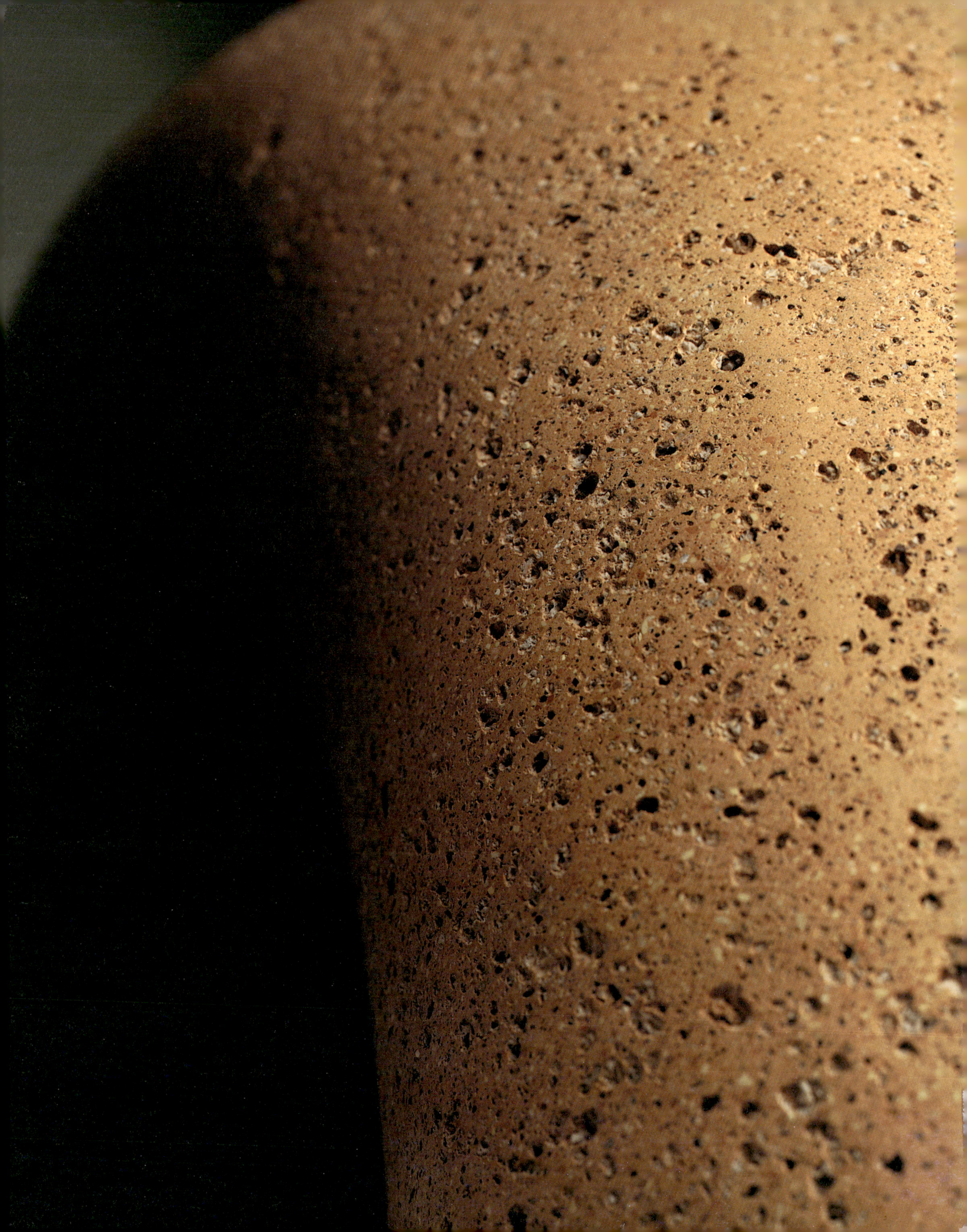